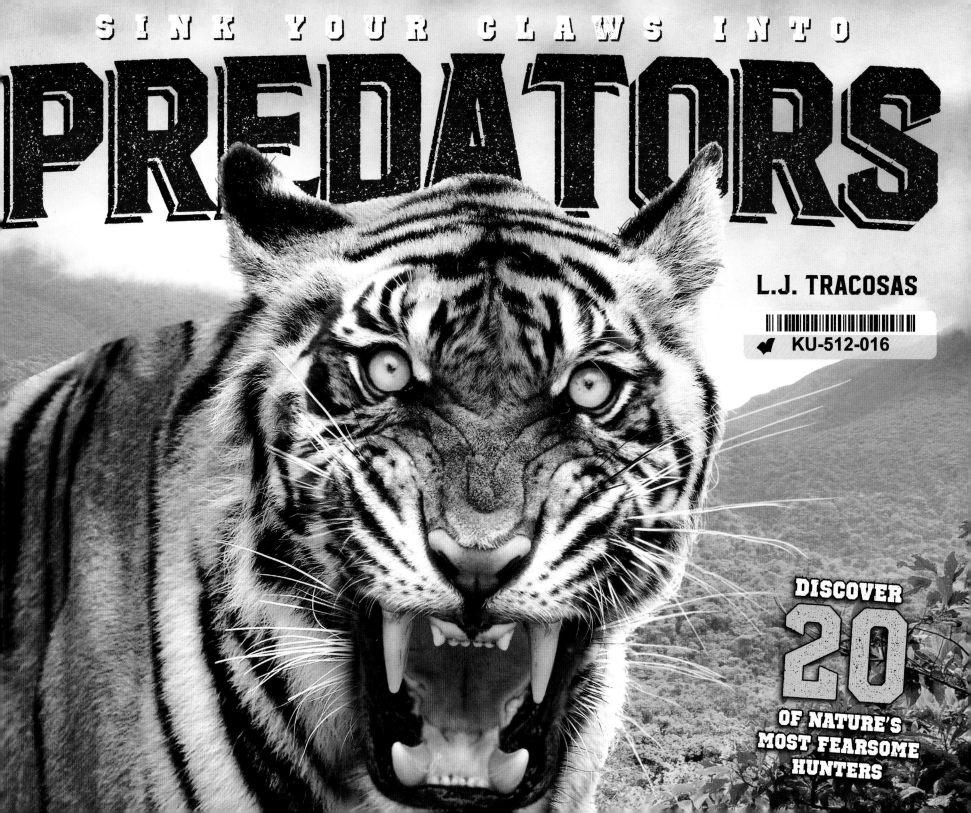

SINK YOUR CLAWS INTO

PREDATORS

L.J. TRACOSAS

DISCOVER
20
OF NATURE'S
MOST FEARSOME
HUNTERS

Sink Your Claws into Predators is produced by becker&mayer!, a division of Quarto Publishing Group USA Inc.

11120 NE 33rd Place, Suite 101

Bellevue, WA 98004

www.quartoknows.com

If you have questions or comments about this product, please visit www.beckermayer.com/customerservice and click on Customer Service Request Form.

Author: L.J. Tracosas
Designers: Sam Dawson and Megan Sugiyama
Editor: Dana Youlin
Photo research: Farley Bookout
Production coordinator: Tom Miller

Printed in Shenzhen, China.

ISBN: 978-1-60380-398-4

12mm

16722

Image credits: COVER: Lion ©Cheryl Ann Quigley/ Shutterstock: Page 3: Tiger growling ©dptro/ Shutterstock; Page 4: Lion growling ©Oleg Troino/ Shutterstock; Grizzly Bear Claws Kenai Alaska USA" ©Laura Duellman/ Shutterstock; Page 5: Wolverine angry Wolverine ©Michal Ninger/ Shutterstock; Portrait of a Royal Bengal tiger alert and staring at the camera ©anekoho/ Shutterstock; American Black Bear ©Gerard Lacz/ AGE Photo; Gray wolf ©blickwinkel / Alamy Stock Photo; Rare elusive Snow Leopard on snow covered hillside" ©Dennis W Donohue/ Shutterstock; Page 6: Bear snatching food in water ©Blaine Harrington/ AGE Photo; Adult Indochinese tigers (Panthera tigris corbetti) fight in the water. ©Dmitry Chulov/ Shutterstock; Page 7: Wolverine climbing branch ©Rfcompany/ AGE Fotostock; Cheetah in Kruger National Park chasing wart hog at full speed ©Dennis W Donohue/ Shutterstock; cat on the white isolated background ©kuban_girl/ Shutterstock; Page 8: Honey Badger ©Philip Bird / Alamy Stock Phot; Page 9: Claw of Honey Badger (Ratel) ©Ewan Chesser/ Shutterstock; Honey Badger ©Ewan Chesser/ Shutterstock; Page 10: Great horned Owl ©Jill Lang/ Shutterstock; Page 11: Great horned Owl claw ©Jill Lang/ Shutterstock; Great horned owl wings spread ©EPG_EuroPhotoGraphics/ Shutterstock; Page 12: American Black Bear ©Gerard Lacz/ AGE Fotostock; Page 13: American Black Bear claw ©Accent Alaska.com / Alamy Stock Photo; Black bear and cub ©Lorraine Logan/ Shutterstock; Page 14: Bengal Tiger ©Sukpaiboonwat/ Shutterstock; Page 15: Tiger Claw ©Tambako the Jaguar/ Getty; bengal tiger handsome ©anekoho/ Shutterstock; Page 16: Gray Wolf ©blickwinkel / Alamy Stock Photo; Page 17: Gray Wolf claw ©Frank Lukasseck/ Getty; Two gray wolves running in snow ©Michelle Lalancette/ Shutterstock; Page 18: Wolverine snarling ©Michal Ninger/ Shutterstock; Page 19: Wolverine claw ©Dennis Jacobsen/ Shutterstock; Wolverine standing on log in snow ©Jim Zuckerman / Alamy Stock Phot; Page 20: Scorpion with claws up ©blickwinkel / Alamy Stock Photo; Page 21: claw of scorpion ©efendy/ Shutterstock; Scorpion in grass ©blickwinkel / Alamy Stock Photo; Page 22: Perigrine falcon ©Stephen Oliver / Alamy Stock Photo; Page 23: Peregrine falcon foot ©Chris Hill/ Shutterstock; Peregrine falcon flying ©Mcarter/ Shutterstock; Page 24: Lion growling ©Oleg Troino/ Shutterstock; Page 25: Lion claw ©Holger Ehlers / Alamy Stock Photo; three lions walking in grass ©Anton_Ivanov/ Shutterstock; Page 26: Tasmanian Devil ©Susan Flashman/ Shutterstock; Page 27: Tasmanian Devil claw ©Susan Flashman/ Shutterstock; Tasmanian Devil ©Adwo/ Shutterstock; Page 28: African Clawed Frog ©Image Quest Marine / Alamy Stock Photo; Page 29: Claw of African Clawed Frog ©blickwinkel / Alamy Stock Photo; African Clawed Frog ©blickwinkel / Alamy Stock Photo; Page 30: Snow Leopard ©Don Johnston_MA / Alamy Stock Photo; Page 31: Snow Leopard claw: Courtesy of Tambako the Jaguar/ Flickr Commons/ https://creativecommons.org/licenses/by-nd/2.0/; Snow Leopard sitting in snow ©Dennis W Donohue/ Shutterstock; Page 32: Grizzly Bear ©Scott E Read/ Shutterstock; Page 33: Grizzly Bear claw ©Laura Duellman/ Shutterstock; Grizzly Bear ©Michal_K/ Shutterstock; Page 34: Fossa ©Fredrik Stenström/ Alamy Stock Photo; Page 35: Fossa claw ©The Africa Image Library / Alamy Stock Photo; Fossa climbing on a rock © Dmitry Shkurin / Alamy Stock Photo; Page 36: Eagle head ©Peter Wey/ Shutterstock; Page 37: Eagle claw ©critterbiz/ Shutterstock; Eagle flying ©rokopix/ Shutterstock; Page 38: Komodo Dragon with mouth open ©Sergey Uryadnikov/ Shutterstock; Page 39: Komodo Dragon claw ©steve estvanik/ Shutterstock; Komodo Dragon ©GUDKOV ANDREY/ Shutterstock; Page 40: Cheetah ©Johan Swanepoel/ Shutterstock; Page 41: Cheetah claw ©Valdecasas/ Shutterstock; Cheetah running ©JonathanC Photography/ Shutterstock; Page 42: Jaguar ©Bedrin/ Shutterstock; Page 43: Jaguar claw: "Courtesy of Tambako The Jaguar/FlickR Commons/ https://creativecommons.org/licenses/by-nd/2.0/"; Jaguar ©Redmond Durrell / Alamy Stock Photo; Page 44: Alligator ©Heiko Kiera/ Shutterstock; Page 45: Alligator claw ©Michael Maes/ Shutterstock; Alligator on log by lake ©Arto Hakola/ Shutterstock; Page 46: Polar Bear ©olga_gl/ Shutterstock; Page 47: Polar Bear claw ©Nagel Photography/ Shutterstock; Polar Bear walking in snow ©BMJ/ Shutterstock; Page 48: Dog Claws ©Igor Normann/ Shutterstock; Sloth with claws ©Seaphotoart/ Shutterstock; face of husky dog ©K.INABA/ Shutterstock; bush babies claws ©Boudewijn Sluijk/ Shutterstock.

Design elements used throughout: reptile vector collection ©Goran J/ Shutterstock; Vector illustration of various cats silhouettes ©oorka/ Shutterstock; ten frog silhouettes ©rachisan alexandra/ Shutterstock; tiger silhouettes and skins-vector ©nemlaza/ Shutterstock; Macro of algae with many little bubbles in aquarium ©waldru/ Shutterstock; Torn paper background with space for text ©totally out/ Shutterstock; Grunge texture - abstract stock vector template ©Milos Djapovic/ Shutterstock; scorpion silhouette on the white background ©yyang/ Shutterstock; Owl set of silhouettes vector ©Airin.dizain/ Shutterstock; Grunge textures backgrounds. Perfect background with space ©Madredus/ Shutterstock; Dotted Abstract Vector ©Miloje/ Shutterstock; Old cracked mossy tree bark ©Volodymyr Tverdokhlib/ Shutterstock; silhouettes of predators ©Niakris6/ Shutterstock; Animal Spoor Footprints ©enjoyeverytime/ Shutterstock; badger silhouettes ©yyang/ Shutterstock; Big cats collection ©Hein Nouwens/ Shutterstock; Australian Dingo Silhouettes ©Zarja/ Shutterstock; Black Scorpion ©Vector Draco/ Shutterstock; Bear Silhouettes ©Nebojsa Kontic/ Shutterstock; Winter fir forest in snow ©Anastasiia Malinich/ Shutterstock; Blue-sky ©Thawornnurak/ Shutterstock; Blue dark night sky ©Pozdeyev Vitaly/ Shutterstock; Blank Blue World map ©vectorEps/ Shutterstock; Wolverine paw print ©LynxVector/ Shutterstock; green trees in a forest of old spruce ©zlikovec/ Shutterstock; Animal tracks and bird footprints ©vectortatu/ Shutterstock; Realistic claw scratches ©MicroOne/ Shutterstock; lonely tree in the middle of the Texas ©AnnaHappy/ Shutterstock.

CONTENTS

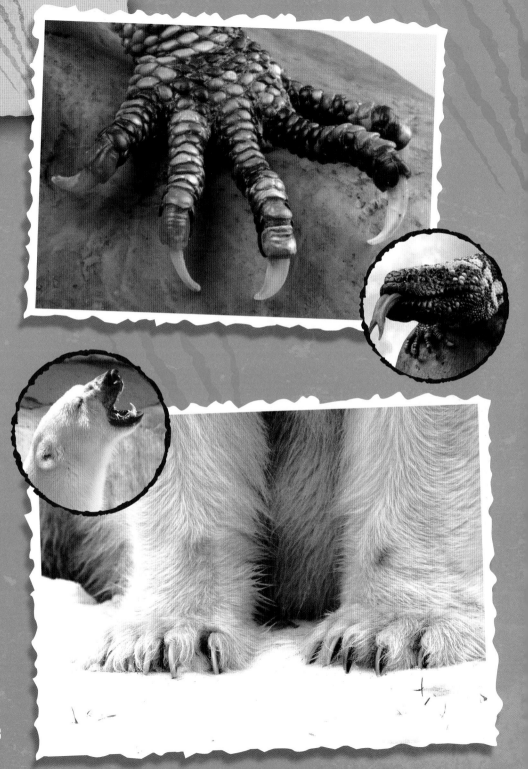

A PLANET OF PREDATORS

Whether it's on land, in the air, or under water, the world is full of predators—or animals that hunt and eat other animals. Predators can be mammals, reptiles, birds, or insects, but all are carnivores—or meat eaters. Predators use different tools to hunt and take down their prey. It could be razor-sharp teeth or a pointed beak, keen eyesight, a super sense of smell or hearing, speed, stealth, smarts, or something entirely different. Mostly it's a combination of these features that makes predators truly amazing hunters.

SHARPENING THEIR CLAWS

One type of weapon that many predators have is claws. Curved and pointed by definition, claws are not your average fingernails—though they are made of the same material, called keratin. Claws are handy for more than just slashing and shredding, though. Animals have come up with many uses for these valuable tools.

WHO'S AT THE TOP?

Many predators are also prey. Even though the scorpion eats other insects and lizards, it can be gobbled up by a snake, a rodent, a bird, or even another scorpion. An apex predator, however, is an animal that is at the top of its food chain, meaning that no other animal preys on it.

WOLVERINE

TIGER

BLACK BEAR

GRAY WOLF

SNOW LEOPARD

SLASHING, CRUSHING, DIGGING IN

There's more than one way to use claws!

SLASHING

Not only can cutting claws be used in an attack, they can also be used as defense. Plenty of predators have to fight against their relatives for territory or protect themselves and their young from other animals.

SNATCHING

Much like predators' teeth, which can be curved, claws can be used for snagging or grasping food that's trying to get away. The curved shape allows for a tight hold for the predator, and a painful escape if the prey does manage to slip out of grip. After all, wounded prey is easier to take down.

CLIMBING

Sure, pointy claws can dig into dinner, but they can also hook into other things, like tree trunks or ice. Many predators use their claws for climbing. Some predators scale trees to get after prey animals looking to escape, and others use them to climb up to a comfy perch.

CHASING

Claws can grip more than prey. They can also grip the ground—something known as traction—and help an animal get more speed and control when running after a meal.

NOW YOU SEE THEM, NOW YOU DON'T

Some claws are always out. This can mean that the sharp ends of the curved nails get worn down by lots of use or constant scraping as the animal moves around.

Retractable claws stay sharp. Retractable means able to pull back, and animals like cats are able to pull their nails back behind a protective layer of skin. This protects the claws from wear and tear, meaning they're super sharp whenever the animal needs them

HONEY BADGER

SCIENTIFIC NAME:
MELLIVORA CAPENSIS

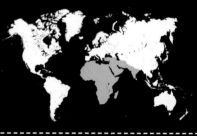

LOCATION: AFRICA, INDIA, AND THE MIDDLE EAST

LENGTH:
29-38 IN (73-96 CM)

WEIGHT:
9-26 LBS (4.1-11.8 KG)

A NOT-SO-SWEET BADGER

With such a sweet name, you might think the honey badger is a nice little critter. Not so! These members of the weasel family are known for pawing beehives, but it's not the honey they're after. Instead, these guys like to eat bee larvae. They also resemble skunks—and not just because of their black bodies and white stripes. Honey badgers also make a stink if they feel threatened. Rather than spraying, they drop what some call a stink bomb on their enemies, which gives them enough time to make their escape.

CLAW FILE #1

Honey badgers' back claws are short, but their front claws are hard to miss. These long nails help the honey badger burrow. They can carve out holes up to 5 feet (1.5 m) deep and dig homes connected by long underground tunnels, measuring up to 9 feet (3 m). Honey badgers also use those fierce nails of theirs to fight predators. They've been seen battling lions, pythons, and hyenas. They're so feisty that the *Guinness Book of World Records* named the honey badger the world's most fearless creature.

GREAT HORNED OWL

SCIENTIFIC NAME:
BUBO VIRGINIANUS

LOCATION: NORTH, CENTRAL, AND SOUTH AMERICA

LENGTH:
1.5-2 FT (0.5-0.6 M)

WINGSPAN:
ABOUT 4.5 FT (1.3M)

WEIGHT:
2-5.5 LBS (1-2.5 KG)

NOT UNICORNS—PLUMICORNS!

Great horned owls don't actually have horns—they just look like they do. The tufts of feathers on each side of their heads resembling cat ears or horns are known as plumicorns. Some scientists think that plumicorns may help the owls blend in with the trees. Like other owls, the great horned owl hunts at night and has large eyes so it can see well in the dark. Its eyeballs are fixed in position, so it can't shift its view without moving its head. Luckily, it can rotate that head in all directions. These big birds of prey feast on small rodents as well as larger rabbits and even geese. Because they don't have teeth to chew with, they gulp down small meals whole—and yak up the bones later.

CLAW FILE #2

Great horned owls have strong legs, and their feet are armed with thick talons. This helps them attack and carry away prey much heavier than themselves. These owls have a thumb-like toe on the outside of each foot. They attack prey from above, then sink their sharp talons into the creature's back and wrap the thumb-like one around the spine, which kills most animals instantly. They also have one talon that's serrated—or has a jagged edge—that they can use for sawing meat.

AMERICAN BLACK BEAR

SCIENTIFIC NAME:
URSUS AMERICANUS

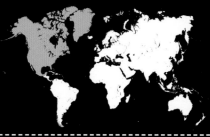

LOCATION: NORTH AMERICA AND MEXICO

LENGTH
6 FT (1.8 M) LONG

WEIGHT:
UP TO 600 LBS (272 KG)

EATING—AND SLEEPING—MACHINES

The American black bear lives in the forests, mountains, and swamps of North America. And it eats almost anything: grasses, leaves, fruits, insects, fish, animals, carrion (or already-dead animals), and even humans' garbage. It eats as much as it can all year until winter arrives. That's when this excellent sleeper dens down to hibernate. The black bear can sleep—and go without food, water, or exercise—for more than 100 days in a row. Now *that's* a nap!

FEATURED CLAW

CLAW FILE #3

American black bears have five toes on each paw, and each toe is tipped with a thick, long claw. The front claws measure about 1.25 inches (3.175 cm). These bears are excellent climbers and are known to scoot up trees as cubs and as adults. Not only do they use their claws to grasp tree trunks but they also use them to pick and grab fruit and grubs to munch.

BENGAL TIGER

SCIENTIFIC NAME:

PANTHERA TIGRIS TIGRIS

LOCATION: INDIA, BANGLADESH, NEPAL, AND BHUTAN

HEIGHT:
7-9 FT (2-3 M), INCLUDING TAIL

WEIGHT:
ABOUT 550 LBS (249 KG)

NO SET OF STRIPES IS ALIKE

The Bengal tiger is one of the biggest of the big cats. These huge felines are ambush—or surprise—hunters, lying silently in wait until unknowing prey wanders near enough. Bengal tigers blend into their surroundings with their special striped coats, and no two tigers have the same pattern of stripes. Their hind legs are longer than their front ones, which gives them extra power to spring. Tigers used to be found throughout Asia, but hunting and damage to their habitats has made it hard for them to survive. There are about 2,500 of these endangered tigers left in the wild.

CLAW FILE #4

Tiger paws are dotted with four knifelike claws that stay protected in a skin covering until they're ready to come out for slashing. The claws can measure up to 4 inches (10 cm) long. Their curved shape helps tigers dig into the flesh of prey like water buffalo and boar and hold on, which makes an attack a success. Tigers also use their claws to climb up trees, but they're useless for climbing back down. These big cats often have to shimmy down a trunk backward, which makes them the worst climbers of the *Panthera* family.

GRAY WOLF

SCIENTIFIC NAME:
CANIS LUPUS

LOCATION: NORTH AMERICA

LENGTH:
4-5.75 FT (1.22-1.67 M),
INCLUDING TAIL

WEIGHT:
40-175 LBS (18-79 KG)

THE BETTER TO EAT YOU WITH!

Even though they're called gray wolves, these canines have coats that can range in color from brown to white to black. This may be because these wolves make their homes in many different habitats, from cold and snow-covered tundra to dry grasslands or deserts to green forests. These hunters work in packs: they join forces with other wolves—usually about nine—and live and hunt together for most of their lives. In one meal, a full-grown wolf can eat up to 20 pounds of meat—that's like eating 80 hamburgers.

CLAW FILE #5

Each of a gray wolf's paws is dotted with four claws that can grow as long as about 2 inches (5 cm). Though these claws are long and strong, gray wolves don't use them for slashing prey, which is usually a big, hoofed animal like an elk. Instead, the claws sink into the ground—kind of like soccer cleats—to give the wolves better grip and speed during a chase.

WOLVERINE

SCIENTIFIC NAME:
GULO GULO

LOCATION: NORTHERN NORTH AMERICA, EUROPE, AND ASIA

LENGTH:
33-44 IN (84-111 CM)

WEIGHT:
24-40 LBS (11-18 KG)

FIT FOR *FROZEN*

The wolverine—the largest animal in the weasel family—is always ready for winter weather. With a thick, greasy coat that repels water and frost, wolverines can live in some seriously cold climates, like arctic tundra. Their special paws spread large with each step to even out the wolverine's weight over snow and ice, almost like snowshoes. They're even born with white coats, which help baby wolverines blend into their snowy surroundings. Those coats eventually turn a dark brown.

CLAW FILE #6

Wolverines mainly use their strong, thick claws for digging. They carve out burrows and dens to live in, and holes for burying food. The nails also help wolverines avoid slipping on ice, acting as crampons—the metal spikes that mountain climbers attach to their boots to give them traction. But of course a wolverine's sharp nails are also helpful for defense and for hunting. Wolverines can take down animals many times their size, such as sickly elk and moose.

RED-CLAWED SCORPION

SCIENTIFIC NAME:
PANDINUS CAVIMANUS

LOCATION: TANZANIA, AFRICA

LENGTH:
3–5 IN (7.6–12.7 CM)

WEIGHT:
UNKNOWN

ANGRY ANTHROPODS

Red-clawed scorpions are also known as Tanzanian reds. They belong to a group of animals called arthropods, which includes insects and crustaceans (like crabs). These particular scorpions live in the hot and humid jungles of Tanzania, in Africa, and hide and hunt in the leaves on the jungle floor. Related to the emperor scorpion, the red-clawed scorpion is one of the largest of its kind. Tanzanian reds are known to be feisty and sting often. Luckily, their venom doesn't hurt more than a bee sting.

CLAW FILE #7

These scorpions get their name from their special red-colored claws, which can be vivid or have just a shade of red. Unlike other scorpions, the red-clawed scorpion doesn't use its venom on prey. So it's big pincers are its main tools for snaring prey, so it's red-clawed scorpions eat insects and small lizards, grabbing and crushing them with their powerful claws.

PEREGRINE FALCON

SCIENTIFIC NAME:
FALCO PEREGRINUS

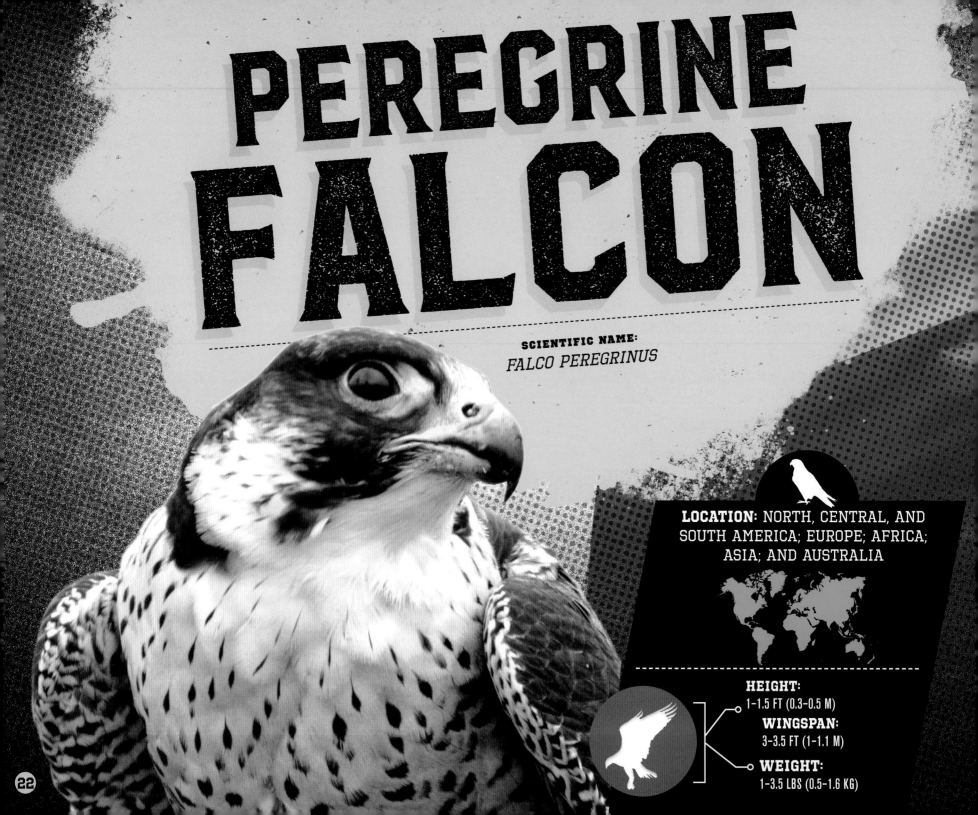

LOCATION: NORTH, CENTRAL, AND SOUTH AMERICA; EUROPE; AFRICA; ASIA; AND AUSTRALIA

HEIGHT:
1–1.5 FT (0.3–0.5 M)

WINGSPAN:
3–3.5 FT (1–1.1 M)

WEIGHT:
1–3.5 LBS (0.5–1.6 KG)

AERIAL ATTACKERS

Peregrine falcons are the fastest birds in the world. These racing raptors—another name for birds of prey—feed on bats and other birds, so they do their hunting in midair. Peregrines soar high above other birds, scanning below them for something in flight. When they spot something with their exceptional eyesight, they dive—and fast. Peregrine falcons have been clocked flying at 200 miles per hour (320 kph) in an attack. *Peregrine* means wanderer, and travel they do. Some falcons have been mapped migrating for more than 15,000 miles per year. That's more than half the distance around the world.

CLAW FILE #8

To snare another bird in midair, you need some serious claws. Peregrine falcons have long, yellow and black talons that are sharp enough to pierce through feather, down, and skin, and strong enough to hold on as the raptor pulls its prey down for dinner. They also use their hooked beaks to shred meat. The hook is called a tomial tooth.

LION

SCIENTIFIC NAME:
PANTHERA LEO

LOCATION: AFRICA

LENGTH:
UP TO 10 FT LONG (3 M),
INCLUDING TAIL

WEIGHT:
UP TO 550 LBS (250 KG)

PANTHERA PRIDE

Known as the king of the jungle, the lion actually prefers grasslands, where it can do plenty of hunting. These top predators live in large groups called prides, which is unique behavior among the big cat family, whose members usually prefer to be alone. Prides range in size from 4 to 30 lions, with mostly females and a few males. Female pride members stick together for life. Remarkable for their big, furry manes—which make them look bigger as well as protect their necks in battles with other lions—the male lions in the group aren't actually the big hunters. They hang out while the female lions work together to hunt for dinner.

CLAW FILE #9

Lions have retractable claws, meaning they're kept pulled back inside the paws until it's time to use them. This keeps the claws razor sharp. On a large lion, the claws can be up to 3 inches (7.6 cm) long. Lions eat large, fast prey, like zebras, and they need their claws to catch their food. Lionesses launch themselves at a running animal and wrap their powerful paws around its neck, sinking their claws in and making it near impossible for the prey to get away.

TASMANIAN DEVIL

SCIENTIFIC NAME:
SARCOPHILUS HARRISII

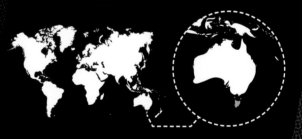

LOCATION: TASMANIA, AUSTRALIA

LENGTH:
20-31 IN (51-79 CM)

WEIGHT:
9-26 LBS (4-12 KG)

ACHOO!

There's no doubt that Tasmanian devils are carnivores. Their love of food is in their scientific name: *Sarcophilus* means meat lover, and these guys will eat pretty much any kind of meat. Snakes, rodents, carrion (the bodies of dead animals)—devils are known as the vacuum cleaners of the forest. These marsupials got their name from their temper. Devils love to fight with each other and other animals—and they make a snarling, growling, and beastly uproar while they're battling. What's their pre-fight ritual? A big sneeze. These guys think it intimidates the competition.

CLAW FILE #10

Devils are born with hooked claws, which they put to use right away. Baby devils—pink, hairless little ones called imps—have to crawl from their mother's birth canal to her pouch (these are marsupials, after all), and they use their already-strong claws to pull themselves along on this journey. When imps become devils, they use their claws for burrowing, digging for food, and holding prey when it tries to get away.

27

AFRICAN CLAWED FROG

SCIENTIFIC NAME:
XENOPUS LAEVIS

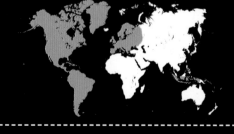

LOCATION: AFRICA, NORTH AND SOUTH AMERICA, EUROPE, AND INDONESIA

LENGTH:
UP TO 4.5 INCHES LONG (10-12 CM)

WEIGHT:
UP TO 7 OZ (200 G)

WHAT ARE WE MISSING?

While the African clawed frog does have claws—an unusual feature among amphibians—it's also missing a few things. These amphibians don't have eyelids. Instead, their eyes are covered with a see-through film. They have no visible ears, though they can hear. They're also missing tongues. Males don't even have vocal sac. They can still communicate, though, by clicking muscles in their throats. African clawed frogs live in still waters and can change their coloring from light to dark to match their surroundings.

CLAW FILE #11

The African clawed frog is named after the spikes on the three inner toes of the frog's back feet. When African clawed frogs are tadpoles, they filter nutrients from the still waters they live in. When they grow up, these hungry frogs will eat anything they can get their claws on. Their three-clawed toes help them grab and hold on to living or dead bugs while they munch away.

SNOW LEOPARD

SCIENTIFIC NAME:
PANTHERA UNCIA

LOCATION: CENTRAL ASIA

LENGTH:
UP TO 8 FT (2.5 M), INCLUDING TAIL

WEIGHT:
60-120 LBS (27-54 KG)

GHOST CATS

These mountain predators are mysterious and hard to study. Snow leopards prefer to be alone and live in harsh, cold, and high-up areas. They stalk mountain goats by perfectly blending in with their surroundings thanks to their white-gray and spotted coats. Because they're so good at hiding, they've earned the nickname "the ghost cats of the Himalayas." Snow leopards have other features, in addition to their coats, that are suited for their tough environment. One is their very long and fluffy tail, which not only helps them balance over rocky ground but also acts as a scarf that they can wrap around themselves and soft body parts like their noses to protect from freezing temperatures.

CLAW FILE #12

Like other big cats, the snow leopard uses its sharp, curved, retractable claws to attack prey. This is especially important in the high mountains where these cats live. Because the cold, rocky areas where they hunt don't feature much room to run, the snow leopard has to use camouflage, silence, and surprise to spring at and catch its prey. Snow leopards are serious leapers: they can jump more than six times their length to sink their claws into prey.

GRIZZLY BEAR

SCIENTIFIC NAME:

URSUS ARCTOS HORRIBILIS

LOCATION: NORTH AMERICA AND ASIA

HEIGHT:
UP TO 8 FT (2.5 M)

WEIGHT:
1300 LBS (599 KG)

LARGE LONERS

Huge and ferocious, grizzly bears are one of the most awesome bears out there. They live and hunt in North America, in the remote areas of Alaska and northwestern Canada, and parts of Asia. Raised in small families with their mothers and siblings, when these big bears grow up, they prefer to go it alone, staying solo rather than joining up, with other bears. If you see one in the wild, give it a lot of space. They've been known to charge and attack humans.

CLAW FILE #13

A grizzly's claws can be up to 6 inches (15.2 cm) long and as thick as a person's finger. Sure, these bears are fierce—one swing of a grizzly's paw could do some serious damage to an animal or person. But these bears mainly use their claws for digging up roots to munch or for dicing up tree logs in search of the tasty bugs that round out the grizzly's mostly vegetarian meals.

FOSSA

SCIENTIFIC NAME:
CRYPTOPROCTA FEROX

LOCATION: MADAGASCAR

LENGTH:
UP TO 6 FT (1.8 M), INCLUDING TAIL

WEIGHT:
15–26.5 LBS (7–12 KG)

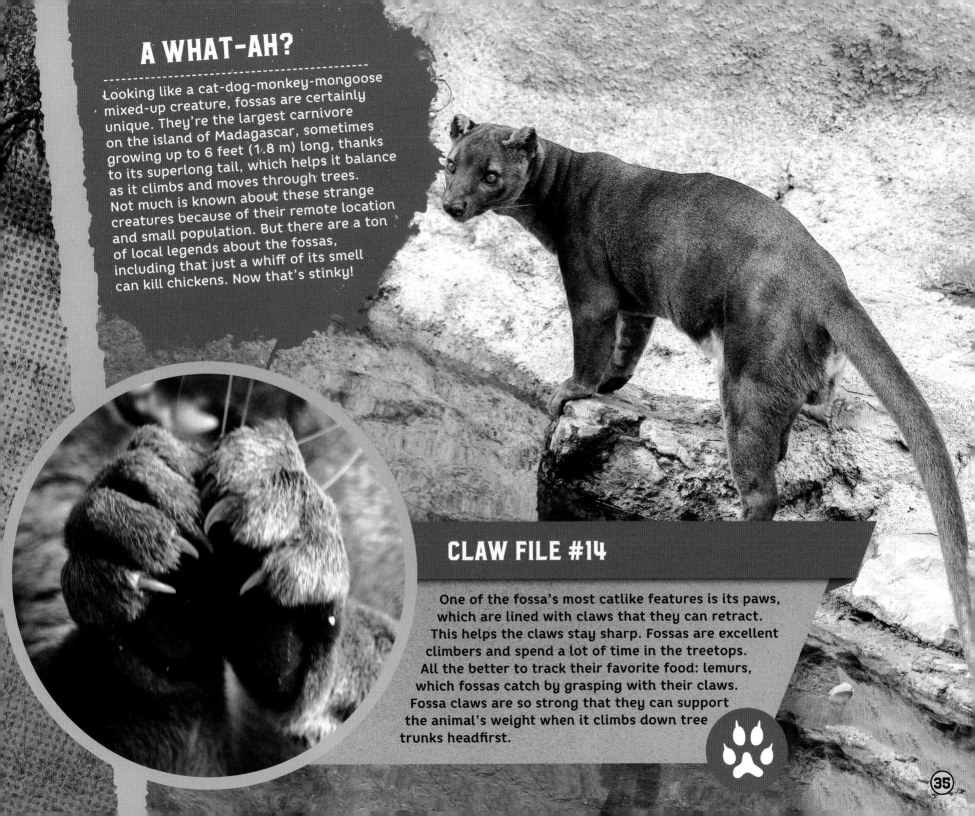

A WHAT-AH?

Looking like a cat-dog-monkey-mongoose mixed-up creature, fossas are certainly unique. They're the largest carnivore on the island of Madagascar, sometimes growing up to 6 feet (1.8 m) long, thanks to its superlong tail, which helps it balance as it climbs and moves through trees. Not much is known about these strange creatures because of their remote location and small population. But there are a ton of local legends about the fossas, including that just a whiff of its smell can kill chickens. Now that's stinky!

CLAW FILE #14

One of the fossa's most catlike features is its paws, which are lined with claws that they can retract. This helps the claws stay sharp. Fossas are excellent climbers and spend a lot of time in the treetops. All the better to track their favorite food: lemurs, which fossas catch by grasping with their claws. Fossa claws are so strong that they can support the animal's weight when it climbs down tree trunks headfirst.

BALD EAGLE

SCIENTIFIC NAME:
HALIAEETUS LEUCOCEPHALUS

LOCATION: NORTH AMERICA

HEIGHT:
3-3.5 FT (0.9-1 M)

WINGSPAN:
6-8 FT (1.8-2.4 M)

WEIGHT:
7-14 LBS (3.1-6.3 KG)

WHO ARE YOU CALLING BALD?

Bald eagles actually have a full head of hair—er, feathers. They're just white, which makes them stand out against the bird's otherwise chocolate-brown-feathered body. The symbol of the United States, these large birds make their homes near water. They often fish for salmon, and sometimes more than 4,000 birds have been seen onshore preparing to feast on the spawning fish. Bald eagles mate for life—meaning they find one partner and stick together—and build nests together. In fact, a pair of bald eagles will continue working on their nest over many years, making these constructions of sticks, leaves, and twigs some of the largest in the world. Bald eagle nests have been measured at up to 10 feet across and 20 feet deep.

FEATURED CLAW

CLAW FILE #15

With a preference for fish, bald eagles need some long, sharp talons for snaring scaly, slippery food. They have three front claws and one back one, called a hallux talon, perfect for gripping. The hallux talon is the longest, measuring up to 2 inches (5 cm) in females. Bald eagles hook fish that are close to the surface of the water and sometimes dive at over 75 mph (120 kph) to catch them. They also steal food from other prey birds, making talons helpful for snatching.

KOMODO DRAGON

SCIENTIFIC NAME:
VARANUS KOMODOENSIS

LOCATION: INDONESIA

LENGTH:
10 FT (3 M)

WEIGHT:
330 LBS (150 KG)

LEAPING LIZARDS

Almost as long as an alligator and weighing as much as a professional wrestler, the Komodo dragon is the largest lizard on the planet. And one of the fiercest, too! These huge reptiles are ambush hunters, meaning they stalk their prey very quietly and wait for the perfect moment to launch a surprise attack. They use their powerful hind legs to leap at prey, which can be anything from deer to pigs to water buffalo. Once they sink their teeth in for even a single chomp, the Komodo dragon's work is done. Their spit contains so many bacteria that even if dinner manages to get away, it'll eventually collapse from the poison.

CLAW FILE #16

Baby Komodo dragons depend on their claws to help them scramble up trees, where they hide for safety until they get bigger. Adult dragons are too big to climb, so they use their claws for other purposes—namely, attacking prey. When the Komodo dragon jumps at its prey, it wraps its powerful arms and legs around the animal to tackle it, snaring it in its grip. It then uses its long claws to rip through the meat.

39

CHEETAH

SCIENTIFIC NAME:
ACINONYX JUBATUS

LOCATION: AFRICA

LENGTH:
5-7 FT (1.5-2 M), INCLUDING TAIL

WEIGHT:
77-143 LBS (35-65 KG)

ON YOUR MARK, GET SET, GO!

Cheetahs are the fastest land animal in the world. They can go from sitting to sprinting at 60 miles per hour in 3 seconds and can cover 20 feet in a single running step. They're able to turn quickly thanks to their claws and their long tails. A cheetah has all of its spots when it's born, so cubs look darker when they're little and lighten as they grow and their spots spread out. These spots help the cheetah hide in the grasslands where they live and hunt. These big felines crouch low and surprise prey like quick gazelles and impala with a sudden burst of speed and a bite to the throat. All that running tires cheetahs out, and they sometimes need to catch their breath for 20 minutes before they can enjoy their dinner.

FEATURED CLAW

CLAW FILE #17

The speedy cheetah uses its strong, blunt claws like cleats. Unlike other big cats, a cheetah can't retract, or pull back, its claws, which means the points are worn down from scraping the ground. So rather than digging into prey, the claws dig into the dirt to help this big cat gain maximum speed. As useful as they are for the chase, claws that aren't sharp may not be helping cheetahs hunt: cheetahs manage to take down only half of the prey they go after.

JAGUAR

SCIENTIFIC NAME:
PANTHERA ONCA

LOCATION: CENTRAL AND SOUTH AMERICA

LENGTH:
7-9 FT (2-3 M), INCLUDING TAIL

WEIGHT:
100-250 LBS (45-113 KG)

SEEING SPOTS

Jaguars are the biggest cats in the Americas, and they can be found in rainforests and jungles. Unlike most felines, jaguars don't mind water and will often take a dip while hunting for fish or caiman (alligator-like creatures). They also eat capybaras (the world's largest rodent) and tapirs, and pretty much any other animals that cross their paths. The jaguar's coat helps it blend in with its surroundings. Jaguars are often confused for leopards because both cats' coats have rosettes, or rose-shaped spots. How to spy the difference? Jaguars have spots within their spots. Sometimes these spots are so close together and the fur underneath so dark that a jaguar can look black, but the spots are there if you look closely enough.

CLAW FILE #18

Curved to a fine point, jaguar claws are sharp and strong. The four claws in each paw retract, or pull back inside a skin covering, until the big cat needs them. Jaguars surprise their prey by silently hiding until prey comes close enough to pounce on. Then they sink their claws in and hold tight with their powerful forearms until they can kill their prey with a powerful bite to the skull. Jaguars also use their claws to shred tree trunks, which they do as one way to mark their territory.

AMERICAN ALLIGATOR

SCIENTIFIC NAME:
ALLIGATOR MISSISSIPPIENSIS

LOCATION: SOUTHERN NORTH AMERICA

LENGTH:
UP TO 15 FT (4.6 M)

WEIGHT:
UP TO 1,000 LBS (453 KG)

KEEPING THE TOOTH FAIRY BUSY

The American alligator is found mostly in the southeastern United States, in states like Florida and Louisiana. Thriving in hot, swampy climates, these crocodile cousins are at the top of their food chain and dine on pretty much everything around them—birds, turtles, fish, snakes, mammals, and every once in a while, people. Alligators have powerful jaws lined with about 80 teeth. Due to constant chomping, the teeth are worn down and fall out regularly. Luckily, they're constantly replaced with new ones. One alligator can go through more than 3,000 teeth in its life.

CLAW FILE #19

Alligators' webbed and scaly feet are tipped with short but sharp claws. Even though they look fierce, the claws are used more for digging than for attacking. Alligators scoop out marsh grasses and mud to form shallow, wet nooks for themselves to camp out in and keep cool. These spaces are sometimes called wallowing holes or gator holes. According to some reports, the claws (along with their tails) are also sometimes used for climbing. Alligators have been known to scale low fences to escape capture.

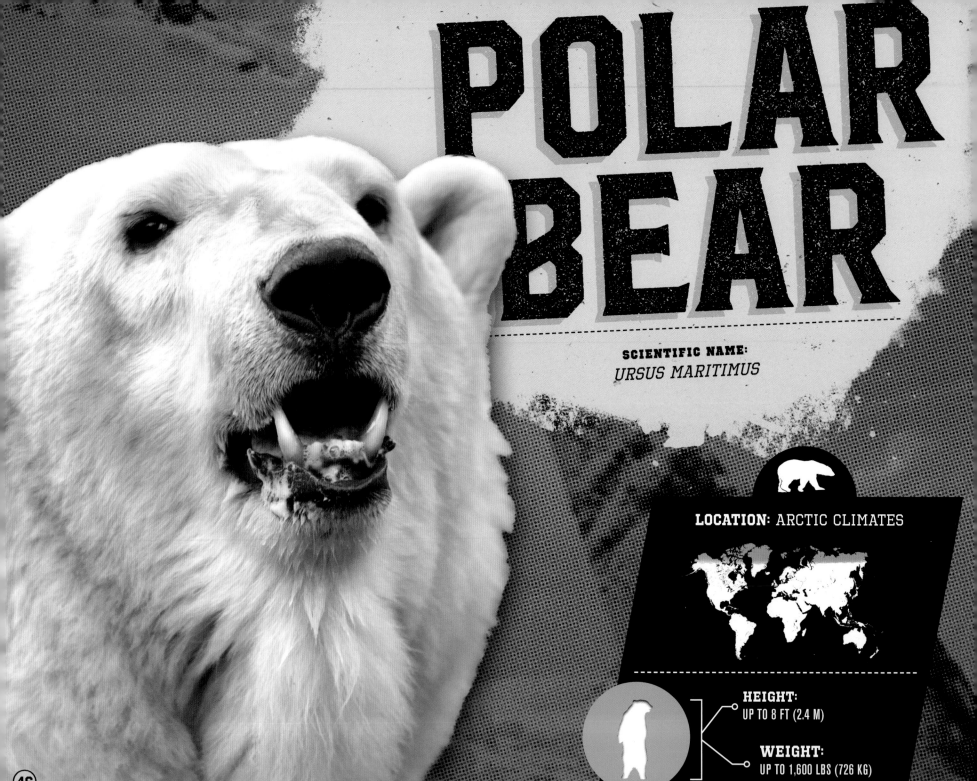

POLAR BEAR

SCIENTIFIC NAME:
URSUS MARITIMUS

LOCATION: ARCTIC CLIMATES

HEIGHT:
UP TO 8 FT (2.4 M)

WEIGHT:
UP TO 1,600 LBS (726 KG)

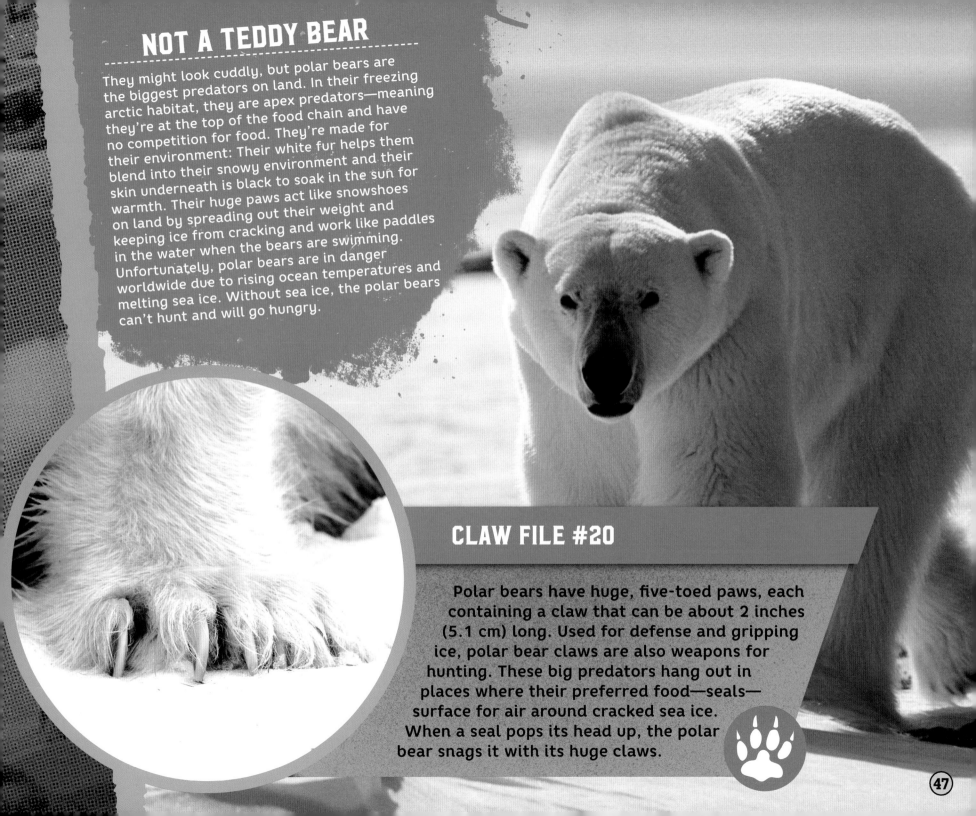

NOT A TEDDY BEAR

They might look cuddly, but polar bears are the biggest predators on land. In their freezing arctic habitat, they are apex predators—meaning they're at the top of the food chain and have no competition for food. They're made for their environment: Their white fur helps them blend into their snowy environment and their skin underneath is black to soak in the sun for warmth. Their huge paws act like snowshoes on land by spreading out their weight and keeping ice from cracking and work like paddles in the water when the bears are swimming. Unfortunately, polar bears are in danger worldwide due to rising ocean temperatures and melting sea ice. Without sea ice, the polar bears can't hunt and will go hungry.

CLAW FILE #20

Polar bears have huge, five-toed paws, each containing a claw that can be about 2 inches (5.1 cm) long. Used for defense and gripping ice, polar bear claws are also weapons for hunting. These big predators hang out in places where their preferred food—seals— surface for air around cracked sea ice. When a seal pops its head up, the polar bear snags it with its huge claws.

CRAZY CLAWS

Predators aren't the only animals who put claws to good use. Check out these other crazy claws!

SUPERLONG CLAWS

Three-toed sloths' superlong claws make it really hard to walk on the ground. But they are perfect for hanging from trees, where sloths spend almost all of their time.

DEWCLAWS

There are claws on the ends of toes, and then there are claws that aren't. Dewclaws are claws that no longer touch the ground. You can find a dewclaw on a dog or cat, on their legs a bit above their paws. Dewclaws are vestigial body parts, or parts of the body that were used in previous generations but no longer are.

TOILET CLAWS

Some animals have claws that are used only for cleaning themselves. For example, bush babies' claws are flatter and not as sharp as other claws, and they use them for grooming their fur.